T0253157

Quotes
for all
Seasons

Quotes
for all
Seasons

OVER 150 QUOTATIONS
FOR YEAR-ROUND
INSPIRATION

Arranged by Jackie Corley

hatherleigh

Hatherleigh Press is committed to preserving
and protecting the natural resources of the earth.
Environmentally responsible and sustainable practices are
embraced within the company's mission statement.

Visit us at www.hatherleighpress.com.

QUOTES FOR
ALL SEASONS

Library of Congress Cataloging-in-Publication Data is available.
ISBN: 978-1-57826-957-0

Cover and Interior Design by Carolyn Kasper

Printed in the United States
10 9 8 7 6 5 4 3 2 1

Winter is an etching,
spring a watercolor,
summer an oil painting, and
autumn a mosaic of them all.

— STANLEY HOROWITZ

CONTENTS

INTRODUCTION

The seasons remind us that change is constant and beauty is abundant. We know that in the deep frost of winter, new life prepares for its future bloom in spring, and on the muggiest, most sweltering day in July, a crisp fall day will return with a pile of leaves underfoot.

Each season brings its own color palette and its own rhythm to our lives. In spring, we celebrate the vibrant color as green leaves sprout from fresh buds and flowers open to the sun. We shake off the dust that settled during the lull in winter and embrace a fresh start. The heat of summer is a time for lazy lounging and pleasure as well as adventure. We take in the sensual overload of its bright colors and lush landscape and enjoy life in the extremes. In fall, bright oranges and deep reds dot our line of vision and the indelible smells of fallen leaves in the crisp air, pumpkin pies and apple cider are seared into memory. Winter is a time to embrace the stillness that comes with the colder months.

This collection celebrates the uniqueness of each season and the way the cyclical change plays out in our own lives.

Spring

Always it's spring and everyone's in
love and flowers pick themselves.

—E. E. CUMMINGS

New Life in Bloom

Spring is the season of new life. Even the deepest, coldest winter comes to an end, as green returns to the world, new buds and fresh flowers spreading everywhere as nature pulls back the covers and prepares to greet the start of a new seasonal cycle.

Spring adds new life and new joy to all that is.

—JESSICA HARRELSON

An optimist is the human personification of spring.

—SUSAN J. BISSONETTE

April is the kindest month. April gets you out of your head and out working in the garden.

—MARTY RUBIN

Behold, my friends, the spring is come; the earth has gladly received the embraces of the sun, and we shall soon see the results of their love!

— SITTING BULL

Despite the heart numbing frost, my soul is blooming like spring.

— DEBASISH MRIDHA

Blossom by blossom the spring begins.

— ALGERNON CHARLES SWINBURNE

But the true nature of the human heart is as whimsical as spring weather. All signals may aim toward a fall of rain when suddenly the skies will clear.

—MAYA ANGELOU

Can words describe the fragrance of the very breath of spring?

—NELTJE BLANCHAN

Despite the forecast, live like it's spring.

—LILLY PULITZER

Every limpid brook is singing
Of the lure of April days;
Every piney glen is ringing
With the maddest roundelays.

Come and let us seek together
Springtime lore of daffodils,
Giving to the golden weather
Greeting on the sun-warm hills.

—LUCY MAUD MONTGOMERY

Come with me into the woods. Where spring is advancing, as it does, no matter what, not being singular or particular, but one of the forever gifts, and certainly visible.

—MARY OLIVER

It is spring again. The earth is like a child that knows poems by heart.

—RAINER MARIA RILKE

It's spring fever. That is what the name of it is. And when you've got it, you want—oh, you don't quite know what it is you do want, but it just fairly makes your heart ache, you want it so!

—MARK TWAIN

It's spring again. I can hear the birds sing again. See the flowers start to bud. See young people fall in love.

—LOU RAWLS

Now every field is clothed with grass, and every tree with leaves; now the woods put forth their blossoms, and the year assumes its gay attire.

—VIRGIL

Spring is a season of the soul to regain its strength.

— LAILAH GIFTY AKITA

Spring is nature's way of saying, 'Let's party!'

— ROBIN WILLIAMS

Spring is painted in daffodil yellows, robin egg blues, new grass green and the brightness of hope for a better life.

— TORI SORENSON

Spring is the best life coach: It gives you all the energy you want, all the positive thoughts you wish and all the boldness you need!

—MEHMET MURAT ILDAN

Spring is the time of plans and projects.

—LEO TOLSTOY

Spring is the time of the year when it is summer in the sun and winter in the shade.

—CHARLES DICKENS

Spring is when life's alive in everything.

—CHRISTINA ROSSETTI

Spring is when you feel like whistling, even with a shoe full of slush.

—DOUG LARSON

Spring makes its own statement, so loud and clear that the gardener seems to be only one of the instruments, not the composer.

—GEOFFREY B. CHARLESWORTH

Spring shows the power and love of the earth; she can grow magnificent flowers from the dirt.

—DEBASISH MRIDHA

Spring unlocks the flowers to paint the laughing soil.

—BISHOP REGINALD HEBER

Spring will come and so will happiness. Hold on. Life will get warmer.

—ANITA KRIZZAN

Spring won't let me stay in this house any longer! I must get out and breathe the air deeply again.

—GUSTAV MAHLER

Spring: an experience in immortality.

—HENRY DAVID THOREAU

Spring's greatest joy beyond a doubt is when it brings the children out.

—EDGAR GUEST

The beautiful spring came, and when nature resumes her loveliness, the human soul is apt to revive also.

— HARRIET ANN JACOBS

The blooming spring is the smile of the ever-joyful nature.

— DEBASISH MRIDHA

The course of the seasons is a piece of clock-work, with a cuckoo to call when it is springtime.

— GEORGE CHRISTOPH LICHTENBERG

The day the Lord created hope was probably the same day he created Spring.

—BERNARD WILLIAMS

The deep roots never doubt spring will come.

—MARTY RUBIN

The pleasures of spring are available to everybody and cost nothing.

—GEORGE ORWELL

The promise of spring's arrival is enough to get anyone through the bitter winter!

—JEN SELINSKY

This is a beautiful time of year with spring beginning to burst forth in many parts of the world, bringing all of its colors, scents, and cheerful sounds. The miracle of the changing seasons, with the reawakening and rebirth in nature, inspires feelings of love and reverence within us for God's marvelous, creative handiwork.

—M. RUSSELL BALLARD

To be interested in the changing seasons is a happier state of mind than to be hopelessly in love with spring.

— GEORGE SANTAYANA

What a strange thing to be alive beneath cherry blossoms.

— KOBAYASHI ISSA

What potent blood hath modest May.

— RALPH WALDO EMERSON

You are reborn with the roses, in every spring.

—JUAN RAMÓN JIMÉNEZ

You can cut all the flowers but you cannot keep spring from coming.

—PABLO NERUDA

Summer

In summer, the song sings itself.

—WILLIAM CARLOS WILLIAMS

Sun & Joyful Abandon

Summer is a time when the world slows down a bit to embrace the heat. The quotes in this section embody the luxury of lazy days lounging in the sun, enjoying the warm weather and the shining memories that are the hallmark of this season.

And so with the sunshine and the great bursts of leaves growing on the trees, just as things grow fast in movies, I had that familiar conviction that life was beginning over again with summer.

— F. SCOTT FITZGERALD

Deep summer is when laziness finds respectability.

— SAM KEEN

Everything good, everything magical happens between the months of June and August.

— JENNY HAN

Green was the silence, wet was the light, the month of June trembled like a butterfly.

—PABLO NERUDA

I have only to break into the tightness of a strawberry, and I see summer—its dust and lowering skies.

—TONI MORRISON

I know that if odor were visible, as color is, I'd see the summer garden in rainbow clouds.

—ROBERT BRIDGES

I love how summer just wraps its arms around you like a warm blanket.

—KELLIE ELMORE

I love summertime more than anything else in the world. That is the only thing that gets me through the winter, knowing that summer is going to be there.

—JACK MCBRAYER

If it could only be like this always—always summer, always alone, the fruit always ripe.

—EVELYN WAUGH

In early June the world of leaf and blade and flowers explode, and every sunset is different.

—JOHN STEINBECK

When the sun is shining, I can do anything; no mountain is too high, no trouble too difficult to overcome.

—WILMA RUDOLPH

In the depth of winter, I finally learned that there was in me an invincible summer.

—ALBERT CAMUS

Live in the sunshine, swim the sea, drink the wild air.

—RALPH WALDO EMERSON

May summer last a hundred years.

—FRANCES MAYES

Oh, the summer night, Has a smile of light, And she sits on a sapphire throne.

—BRYAN PROCTER

One benefit of summer was that each day we had more light to read by.

—JEANNETTE WALLS

One must maintain a little bit of summer, even in the middle of winter.

—HENRY DAVID THOREAU

Rejoice as summer should ... chase away sorrows by living.

—MELISSA MARR

Rest is not idleness, and to lie sometimes on the grass on a summer day listening to the murmur of water, or watching the clouds float across the sky, is hardly a waste of time.

—JOHN LUBBOCK

Some of the best memories are made in flip-flops.

—KELLIE ELMORE

Spring being a tough act to follow, God created June.

—AL BERNSTEIN

Spring has many American faces. There are cities where it will come and go in a day and counties where it hangs around and never quite gets there. Summer is drawn blinds in Louisiana, long winds in Wyoming, shade of elms and maples in New England.

—ARCHIBALD MACLEISH

Summer afternoon—summer afternoon; to me those have always been the two most beautiful words in the English language.

—HENRY JAMES

Summer ends, and Autumn comes, and he who would have it otherwise would have high tide always and a full moon every night.

—HAL BORLAND

Summer has a flavor like no other. Always fresh and simmered in sunshine.

—OPRAH WINFREY

Summer has filled her veins with light and her heart is washed with noon.

—C. DAY LEWIS

Summer is singing with joy, and the beaches are inviting you with dancing waves.

—DEBASISH MRIDHA

Summer is the annual permission slip to be lazy. To do nothing and have it count for something. To lie in the grass and count the stars. To sit on a branch and study the clouds.

—REGINA BRETT

Summer is the time when one sheds one's tensions with one's clothes, and the right kind of day is jeweled balm for the battered spirit. A few of those days and you can become drunk with the belief that all's right with the world.

— ADA LOUISE HUXTABLE

Summer means happy times and good sunshine. It means going to the beach, going to Disneyland, having fun.

— BRIAN WILSON

Summer's lease hath all too short a date.

— WILLIAM SHAKESPEARE

Summertime is always the best of what might be.

— CHARLES BOWDEN

The dandelions and buttercups gild all the lawn: the drowsy bee stumbles among the clover tops, and summer sweetens all to me.

— JAMES RUSSELL LOWELL

The grill is the summer equivalent of a fireplace; everyone gravitates to it.

— KATIE LEE

The softness of the summer day like an ermine paw.

—ANAÏS NIN

The summer night is like a perfection of thought.

—WALLACE STEVENS

There shall be eternal summer in the grateful heart.

—CELIA THAXTER

To see the summer sky is poetry, though never in a book it lie—true poems flee.

—EMILY DICKINSON

Wander a whole summer if you can. Time will not be taken from the sum of life. Instead of shortening, it will definitely lengthen it and make you truly immortal.

—JOHN MUIR

Warm summer sun, shine kindly here.

—MARK TWAIN

Autumn

Every leaf speaks bliss to me,
fluttering from the autumn tree.

—EMILY BRONTË

Rich Color
& Crisp Air

Autumn brings cooler temperatures and paints the world in deeper, richer tones. The quotes found in this section celebrate the fall leaves, the holiday traditions of harvest time, and the beauty found in the quieter moments as the world begins to wind down.

And when you take something like the changing colour of autumn leaves and start to ask why; you're starting off on an intellectual journey which will take you beyond that moment of visual satisfaction while robbing nothing from that experience.

—ALICE ROBERTS

Anyone who thinks fallen leaves are dead has never watched them dancing on a windy day.

—SHIRA TAMIR

As long as autumn lasts, I shall not have hands, canvas and colors enough to paint the beautiful things I see.

—VINCENT VAN GOGH

Autumn arrives in early morning, but spring at the close of a winter day.

—ELIZABETH BOWEN

Autumn carries more gold in its pocket than all the other seasons.

—JIM BISHOP

Autumn flings her fiery cloak over the sumac, beech and oak.

—SUSAN LENDROTH

Autumn is a second spring when every leaf is a flower.

—ALBERT CAMUS

Autumn is the mellower season, and what we lose in flowers we more than gain in fruits.

—SAMUEL BUTLER

Autumn is the time when nature takes her watercolor to the trees.

—LAURA JAWORSKI

Autumn leaves are falling, filling up the streets; golden colors on the lawn, nature's trick or treat!

—RUSTY FISCHER

Autumn leaves don't fall, they fly. They take their time and wander on this their only chance to soar.

—DELIA OWENS

Autumn mornings: sunshine and crisp air, birds and calmness, year's end and day's beginnings.

—TERRI GUILLEMETS

Autumn wins you best by this its mute appeal to sympathy for its decay.

—ROBERT BROWNING

Autumn, the year's last, loveliest smile.

—WILLIAM C. BRYANT

Change is a measure of time and, in the autumn, time seems speeded up. What was is not and never again will be; what is is change.

— EDWIN WAY TEALE

Delicious autumn! My very soul is wedded to it, and if I were a bird I would fly about the earth seeking the successive autumns.

— GEORGE ELIOT

Fall has always been my favorite season. The time when everything bursts with its last beauty, as if nature had been saving up all year for the grand finale.

— LAUREN DESTEFANO

I loved autumn, the one season of the year that God seemed to have put there just for the beauty of it.

— LEE MAYNARD

How beautiful the leaves grow old. How full of light and color are their last days.

—JOHN BURROUGHS

I notice that Autumn is more the season of the soul than of nature.

—FRIEDRICH NIETZSCHE

If a year was tucked inside of a clock, then autumn would be the magic hour.

—VICTORIA ERICKSON

Is not this a true autumn day? Just the still melancholy that I love—that makes life and nature harmonize.

—GEORGE ELIOT

Life is a dream and autumn is a dream within dream!

—MEHMET MURAT ILDAN

Life starts all over again when it gets crisp in the fall.

—F. SCOTT FITZGERALD

No spring nor summer beauty hath such grace
as I have seen in one autumnal face.

—JOHN DONNE

October is the fallen leaf, but it is also a wider
horizon more clearly seen. It is the distant
hills once more in sight, and the enduring
constellations above them once again.

—HAL BORLAND

The fallen leaves in the forest seemed to make
even the ground glow and burn with light.

—MALCOLM LOWRY

The heat of autumn is different from the heat of summer. One ripens apples, the other turns them to cider.

—JANE HIRSHFIELD

The most beautiful carpet is the carpet made of autumn leaves!

—MEHMET MURAT ILDAN

The tints of autumn...a mighty flower garden blossoming under the spell of the enchanter, frost.

—JOHN GREENLEAF WHITTIER

There is a harmony in autumn, and a lustre in its sky, which through the summer is not heard or seen, as if it could not be, as if it had not been!

—PERCY BYSSHE SHELLEY

There is something incredibly nostalgic and significant about the annual cascade of autumn leaves.

—JOE L. WHEELER

Of all the seasons, autumn offers the most to man and requires the least of him.

—HAL BORLAND

When the autumn meets the tranquility, there you can see the King of the Sceneries!

—MEHMET MURAT ILDAN

When you are reluctant to change, think of the beauty of autumn.

—VV BROWN

Why is it that so many of us persist in thinking that autumn is a sad season? Nature has merely fallen asleep, and her dreams must be beautiful if we are to judge by her countenance.

— SAMUEL TAYLOR COLERIDGE

Wild is the music of the autumnal winds amongst the faded woods.

— WILLIAM WORDSWORTH

Winter

─────────────

Winter is not a season, it's a celebration.

— ANAMIKA MISHRA

A Snowy
Wonderland

Winter is a time when he hunker down and enjoy the stillness of a snowy wonderland. Quotes in this section will focus on the beauty of winter as well as the appreciation it gives us for the warmer and easier seasons throughout the year.

A snow day literally and figuratively falls from the sky—unbidden—and seems like a thing of wonder.

— SUSAN ORLEAN

I know the look of an apple that is roasting and sizzling on the hearth on a winter's evening, and I know the comfort that comes of eating it hot, along with some sugar and a drench of cream ... I know how the nuts taken in conjunction with winter apples, cider, and doughnuts, make old people's tales and old jokes sound fresh and crisp and enchanting.

— MARK TWAIN

He who marvels at the beauty of the world in summer will find equal cause for wonder and admiration in winter.

—JOHN BURROUGHS

How many lessons of faith and beauty we should lose, if there were no winter in our year!

—THOMAS WENTWORTH HIGGINSON

I know a little more how much a simple thing like a snowfall can mean to a person.

—SYLVIA PLATH

Despite all I have seen and experienced, I still get the same simple thrill out of glimpsing a tiny patch of snow.

— EDMUND HILLARY

I love snow for the same reason I love Christmas. It brings people together while time stands still.

— RACHEL COHN

I pray this winter be gentle and kind—a season of rest from the wheel of the mind.

—JOHN GEDDES

I prefer winter and fall, when you feel the bone structure of the landscape — the loneliness of it; the dead feeling of winter. Something waits beneath it, the whole story doesn't show.

—ANDREW WYETH

I wonder if the snow loves the trees and fields that it kisses them so gently? And then it covers them up snug, you know, with a white quilt; and perhaps it says, 'Go to sleep, darlings, till the summer comes again.'

— LEWIS CARROLL

If we had no winter, the spring would not be so pleasant: if we did not sometimes taste of adversity, prosperity would not be so welcome.

— ANNE BRADSTREET

In seed time learn, in harvest teach, in winter enjoy.

—WILLIAM BLAKE

In winter, I plot and plan. In spring, I move.

—HENRY ROLLINS

It is the life of the crystal, the architect of the flake, the fire of the frost, the soul of the sunbeam. This crisp winter air is full of it.

—JOHN BURROUGHS

January brings the snow, makes our feet and fingers glow.

— SARA COLERIDGE

Let us love winter, for it is the spring of genius.

— PIETRO ARETINO

No winter lasts forever; no spring skips its turn.

— HAL BORLAND

O, wind, if winter comes, can spring be far behind?

—PERCY BYSSHE SHELLEY

Snow falling soundlessly in the middle of the night will always fill my heart with sweet clarity.

—NOVALA TAKEMOTO

Snow isn't just pretty. It also cleanses our world and our senses, not just of the soot and grime of a mining town, but also of a kind of weary familiarity, a taken-for-granted quality to which our eyes are all too susceptible.

—JOHN BURNSIDE

That's what winter is: an exercise in remembering how to still yourself then how to come pliantly back to life again.

—ALI SMITH

Surely everyone is aware of the divine pleasures which attend a wintry fireside; candles at four o'clock, warm hearthrugs, tea, a fair tea-maker, shutters closed, curtains flowing in ample draperies to the floor, whilst the wind and rain are raging audibly without.

— THOMAS DE QUINCEY

Thank goodness for the first snow, it was a reminder—no matter how old you became and how much you'd seen, things could still be new if you were willing to believe they still mattered.

— CANDACE BUSHNELL

Snowflakes are winter's butterflies.

—AUTHOR UNKNOWN

The color of springtime is in the flowers; the color of winter is in the imagination.

—TERRI GUILLEMETS

The fire is winter's fruit.

—ARABIAN PROVERB

The first fall of snow is not only an event, it is a magical event. You go to bed in one kind of a world and wake up in another quite different.

—J.B. PRIESTLEY

The flowers of late winter and early spring occupy places in our hearts well out of proportion to their size.

—GERTRUDE S. WISTER

There's just something beautiful about walking on snow that nobody else has walked on. It makes you believe you're special.

—CAROL RIFKA BRUNT

To appreciate the beauty of a snowflake it is necessary to stand out in the cold.

—ARISTOTLE

To keep a warm heart in winter is the real victory.

—MARTY RUBIN

Welcome, winter. Your late dawns and chilled breath make me lazy, but I love you none-theless.

—TERRI GUILLEMETS

What good is the warmth of summer, without the cold of winter to give it sweetness.

—JOHN STEINBECK

Winter forms our character and brings out our best.

—TOM ALLEN

Winter is a season of recovery and preparation.

— PAUL THEROUX

Winter is the time for comfort, for good food and warmth, for the touch of a friendly hand and for a talk beside the fire: it is the time for home.

— EDITH SITWELL

Winter, a lingering season, is a time to gather golden moments, embark upon a sentimental journey, and enjoy every idle hour.

—JOHN BOSWELL

You can't get too much winter in the winter.

—ROBERT FROST

Changes

I think that to one in sympathy with nature,
each season, in turn, seems the loveliest.

—MARK TWAIN

A Time for
Every Season

The changing seasons give us an appreciation that nothing lasts forever and that life is a continuous circle. Stopping to appreciate the beauty not just of each season individually, but the timeless cycle they move through year after year, lets us glimpse the majesty of our world.

Celebrate each season, for you too, are transformed with the turns of the earth.

— ARTHUR DOBRIN

Every season has a reason. Summer cannot do the works of winter, nor winter the works of summer. Each season is unique yet so important, so cherish the seasons in your life.

— GIFT GUGU MONA

Every season has its peaks and valleys. What you have to try to do is eliminate the Grand Canyon.

— ANDY VAN SLYKE

Expect to have hope rekindled. The dry seasons in life do not last. The spring rains will come again.

— SARAH BAN BREATHNACH

I believe in process. I believe in four seasons. I believe that winter's tough, but spring's coming. I believe that there's a growing season. And I think that you realize that in life, you grow. You get better.

— STEVE SOUTHERLAND

I need the seasons to live to the rhythm of rain and sun.

— SOPHIE MARCEAU

I trust in nature for the stable laws of beauty and utility. Spring shall plant and autumn garner to the end of the time.

— ROBERT BROWNING

It is a maxim universally agreed upon in agriculture, that nothing must be done too late; and again, that everything must be done at its proper season; while there is a third precept which reminds us that opportunities lost can never be regained.

— PLINY THE ELDER

Just as the seasons change and the honeybees pollinate the planet and make honey, we are also doing exactly what we are supposed to be doing. We also are a part of nature, certainly not separate from nature.

—BRYAN KEST

Live each season as it passes; breathe the air, drink the drink, taste the fruit, and resign yourself to the influences of each.

—HENRY DAVID THOREAU

Look to the seasons when choosing your cures.

—HIPPOCRATES

Love the trees until their leaves fall off, then encourage them to try again next year.

—CHAD SUGG

Merely having seen the season change in a country gave one the sense of having been there for a long time.

—WILLA CATHER

Each new season grows from the leftovers from the past. That is the essence of change, and change is the basic law.

—HAL BORLAND

Nature gives to every time and season some beauties of its own; and from morning to night, as from the cradle to the grave, it is but a succession of changes so gentle and easy that we can scarcely mark their progress.

—CHARLES DICKENS

Spring is the fountain of love for thirsty winter.

—MUNIA KHAN

Spring passes and one remembers one's
innocence.

Summer passes and one remembers one's
exuberance.

Autumn passes and one remembers one's
reverence.

Winter passes and one remembers one's
perseverance.

—YOKO ONO

The coming and going of the seasons give us more than the springtimes, summers, autumns, and winters of our lives. It reflects the coming and going of the circumstances of our lives like the glassy surface of a pond that shows our faces radiant with joy or contorted with pain.

— GARY ZUKHAV

The leaves fall, the wind blows, and the farm country slowly changes from the summer cottons into its winter woods.

— HENRY BESTON

The seasons are what a symphony ought to be:
four perfect movements in harmony with each
other.

—ARTHUR RUBINSTEIN

The seasons change their manners, as the year
had found some months asleep and leapt them
over.

—WILLIAM SHAKESPEARE

The sun shines different ways in winter and summer. We shine different ways in the seasons of our lives.

—TERRI GUILLEMETS

There are places and climates, seasons and hours, with their outward circumstance, so much in harmony with certain impressions of the heart, that Nature and the soul of man appear to be parts of one vast whole.

—ALPHONSE DE LAMARTINE

There is a season for everything under the sun—even when we can't see the sun.

—JARED BROCK

To be interested in the changing seasons is a happier state of mind than to be hopelessly in love with spring.

—GEORGE SANTAYANA

We cannot stop the winter or the summer from coming. We cannot stop the spring or the fall or make them other than they are. They are gifts from the universe that we cannot refuse. But we can choose what we will contribute to life when each arrives.

— GARY ZUKHAV

When the seasons change, we experience a sympathetic internal shift. All life forms open themselves up to receive cosmic redirection from nature during these crucial seasonal transitions, so we are likely to be more vulnerable and unsettled.

— MAYA TIWARI

When the seasons shift, even the subtle beginning, the scent of a promised change, I feel something stir inside me. Hopefulness? Gratitude? Openness? Whatever it is, it's welcome.

—KRISTIN ARMSTRONG

When you're young you prefer the vulgar months, the fullness of the seasons. As you grow older you learn to like the in-between times, the months that can't make up their minds. Perhaps it's a way of admitting that things can't ever bear the same certainty again.

—JULIAN BARNES

Winter is an etching, spring a watercolor, summer an oil painting, and autumn a mosaic of them all.

— STANLEY HOROWITZ

You expected to be sad in the fall. Part of you died each year when the leaves fell from the trees and their branches were bare against the wind and the cold, wintry light. But you knew there would always be the spring, as you knew the river would flow again after it was frozen.

— ERNEST HEMINGWAY

CONCLUSION

F ROM THE RENEWAL OF life in springtime to the burst of colors in autumn, from the brilliant sunshine of summertime to the quiet snowfalls in winter, there is something in the changing of the seasons that captures our hearts and our imaginations. As the seasons change, so, too do we—becoming more vibrant and outgoing as summer approaches, becoming more contemplative and introspective as winter comes. The four seasons represent a fundamental truth about life on this planet: that every change, no matter what form it takes, hides within it some form of beauty. We just need to take the time to look for it.